THE
# LONG AGO
POEMS

# THE
# LONG AGO
# POEMS

## VLADIMIR AZAROV

**EXILE**
editions

singular fiction, poetry, nonfiction, translation, drama, and graphic books
2024

Library and Archives Canada Cataloguing in Publication

Title: The long ago poems / Vladimir Azarov.
Names: Azarov, Vladimir, 1935- author.
Identifiers: Canadiana 2024048567X | ISBN 9781990773266 (softcover)
Subjects: LCGFT: Poetry.

Book designed by Michael Callaghan
Typeset in Bembo and Birka fonts at Moons of Jupiter Studios

Published by Exile Editions Ltd ~ www.ExileEditions.com
   144483 Southgate Road 14, Holstein, Ontario, N0G 2A0
Printed and Bound in Canada by Marquis

Canadä  ONTARIO CREATES

We gratefully acknowledge the  Government of Canada and Ontario Creates for
   their financial support toward our publishing activities.

Canadian sales representation: The Canadian Manda Group, 664 Annette Street,
Toronto ON M6S 2C8 www.mandagroup.com 416 516 0911

North American and international distribution, and U.S. sales:
Independent Publishers Group, 814 North Franklin Street,
Chicago IL 60610 www.ipgbook.com toll free: 1 800 888 4741

*The insect is tired. The noise and the bright
lights gave it hallucinations. Please be calm.
It's nothing at all. It will recover tomorrow*

—THE BEDBUG, VLADIMIR MAYAKOVSKY

# KAFKA and KHRUSCHEV

*Als Gregor Samsa eines Morgens aus unruhigen Träumen
erwachte, fand er sich in seinem Bett zu einem ungeheuren
Ungeziefer verwandelt.*
—F. KAFKA

Kafka, in a row of books
brought from my library in Moscow.
It was Pasternak who gave Kafka in
translation to Akhmatova who said: "He wrote
for me and about me…"


A dream: … eyes opening at
a knock, that dreaded knock on the door in the night!
Except this was in the morning. The dread was
real, dread in the morning light of
my Moscow rooms… 14 square metres close by
Paveletsky Station, Mayakovsky's stop (home base
for Bedbugs—"a catacomb
of the soul, a skull brimful of verse").
Yes, the knock!
"What's happened? Who is at the door?"
"Frau Gruber."
"Who are you?
Maybe it's my friend, Alisa, the poet pulling my leg,
pretending to be someone else. Often it is
necessary to pretend to achieve an air of normalcy.
Whatever that is.

No! Not Alisa. Too early!

The door opens.

     "Frau Gruber."

     "I've brought you happiness! Kafka!"

     " In your mad hands?"

"'Kafka' in Cyrillic on a black cover! Malevich black."

     "You've got to be happy. In the whole of the USSR, there's only 60,000 copies. THEY—such scum—THEY are (waving her fist in my 14 metre room!), THEY are our awful apparatchiks, THEY sent 6,000 copies to those dimwitted Kafkian Czechs. Maybe a few more for Soviet officers. Complete dullards. Our stupid Ministry of Culture— a fluttering of her hands at my ceiling! Our country is only getting worse, more and more boring. We are a living still life by Braque. No, no, wrong. Worse. We are still."

     "Frau Gruber…you're a born dissident, but the price you require in your fist is half my monthly salary. I'll pay, of course, but it is half."

     "Then you are making big money at your work!"

     "I work with your apparatchicks. It's not easy."

     "THEY…"

     "Me, you and THEY are pure Kafka!"

     *"A book must be an ax for the frozen sea within us.'"*

We entered a Kafkian metamorphosis in the '60s!
A see-saw, helter-skelter time. Insects crawling into the sun, shining.

Like the insect in Khrushchev's Italian left shoe!

(Our Soviet leader had looked the Big Insect in the eye and survived. So sinister himself, murderous, saying he felt a certain itchy-crawling between his toes, remembered from his peasant boyhood.)

His menacing smile. Our man in the politburo.

Was he losing control? His leadership?

I think not. But rot. Yes,
at full throttle the rot had set in.

*Go away, go away insidious Bug!*

In a stage whisper aimed at international apparatchiks assembled (what else) in the Assembly, moving his left shoe to his right hand, he bangs his handmade Via Condotti shoe
(a Bedbug skitters)
hard on the United Nations desk! The heel. The toe in the grip of his fist. Bang. Bang. *Gthunk*. Wild. The world media went wild—our knuckle-duster politician! At work.

Still, in our landscape, where laughter could mean a life
sentence, he is my favourite—

As Controller of the Castle,  for reasons unknown,
he let my father out of the Gulag!

## THE CHANGING LIGHT

A five-hour flight. An American city.
Mysterious light. Ocean's dark sheen.
Seen by the Light of Ferlinghetti's
Coney Island of the Mind.

My heart sinking, a turbulence—
Empty-eyed sky. No moon at all. Coming in for landing.
Oblique space. Chain lines of street lights.
The cross hairs of a city's layout.

Airport. Taxi. A driver who cannot speak English.
Opens the door. I can hardly speak English. I'm inside.
Cocooned. Embracing a back seat darkness.
The arcing of overhead owl lights.

The cab begins to fly, then falls, then flies…
up-and-down streets! The far hills are where home now is.
Green! Go. Disappear into an abyss of unknowingness!

I am dizzy… The Cab is
chasing a Poet's Changeling Light…

It is the Poet's birthday. The Great Ferlinghetti!
Did you not, Lawrence, invite my pal, my buddy,
my co-student of architecture in Moscow,
Voznesensky, Andrei,
        to San Francisco?

You were his companion at the Sydney Opera!

My Andrei, and your Allen. Together. Me, by proxy. Dreaming.

There, in your Kuribayashi camera, all of you were upside down…

Ginsberg the Howler of our time. Upside down. Snap. Snap.
Over and over. Upside down, howling for posterity.
His beard hanging, upended.

Managing to smile his celluloid smile.

Oh, Ferlinghetti! You said:

"I am waiting for my case to come up!"
Sardonic. Paranoid. Playful?
What did that mean? How could I know?

"Let it be." So the Beatles said.

Driver! Why did you stop? What's gone wrong?
I have my passport, my papers, they're in order.

My hotel?
A burning burning burning inscription
MARRIOT
in the dark sky,
the moonless abyss!

Thanks! Here's your tip, five dollars, American.
See, how quickly I get the hang of it here.
Tip, on the tip of... what?

## SAMOVAR ONE

The Yerba Buene Gardens lounge. I am
at a marble top table...
drinking herbal tea
from a San Francisco samovar...
so glad to taste the local aromatic drink;

it's not the usual beer vodka wine whisky bar—
no—it's a TEA LOUNGE.
I have entered into this Pacific
Coast to be greeted by a Turner
hyper-realistic watercolour—

I am tired—
but something revolutionary is
hanging from the ceiling—a fan that is
moving counter-clockwise. This cannot be.
But to my eye, it is. You are too trusting,
I tell myself: be careful, don't become
your own worst enemy. You are
by nature amiable.

At a nearby table
several people are hotly discussing... what?
I am in the Bay City, my first day,
A turbulence of discussion; I am used to
measured words, warily chosen words,
the passion is in the measurement.
while my café neighbour—

(as it turns out) is/was—Harvey Milk!

His backpack is on the floor (his hump of pain?)
just in from New York:

—it is 1972—so long ago—
his revolution beginning… and he,
Harvey, how could he ever foresee that he will be killed?
Murdered.

At Yerba Buene Gardens Tea Lounge,
at a marble top table,

        I am, sipping a cup of herbal tea
from a San Francisco Samovar
though I'm not much of a tea drinker

and it's not much of a samovar
in this town of heated discussions, for sure,
but also where, I can see,
money does the real talking
because I hear someone say with finality,
"Show me the money."

## SAMOVAR TWO

Crystal-clean, transparent, translucent—
this glass teapot… a SAMOVAR!
in San Francisco! Pleasant, curious!
NOT a copper cistern like a Russian SAMOVAR—

with a LEATHER BOOT
on top working as a bellows

to rouse a fire, like a church organ, pumping, pumping!
No, this glass teapot doesn't need a big fire;

this is an American high-tech brewer—something
pristine about it—unsullied—that they call a SAMOVAR.

It comes from San Francisco's MOMA—
owner of a Kazimir Malevich cubist painting—
SAMOVAR!

I ask, and Malevich replies:

"Vladimir… not so long ago I studied with
VKhuTeMas ( stepping stones to Bauhaus,
Higher Art And Technical Studies) in
Moscow—incubator of the Russian avant-garde…

Oh, Vladimir, I forgive you—yes I do, now, as you
stare at my canvas in this oddly alien
San Francisco museum,
all my zigs and zags, triangles, squares, and dotted lines—

Did you watch the water boil in the samovar? No? Hmm..."

Sorry, Kazimir!
When I was a student, everything was different—
you were our aesthetic sanctuary—hiding out
in your black square, we were released!

There were no glass samovars: no wrong-
headed replicas; no exercises in efficiencies
that will always break down;
your SAMOVAR was our underground,
quietly, insidiously subversive: it was real,
pumped by the required bellows.

## O MADELEINE!

O Mary!
Witness to His Crucifixion,
dark flower of affirmation at the foot of the Cross.
His death commemorated by Christmas
pastries: they are in your Name,
Beautiful, mouth-watering cookies—
baked by that Army for the Lord, the Jesuits…
the Society of Jesus and their
sweet MADELEINES.

> *See this woman? I came*
> *Into your house and you gave me no water for my feet,*
> *But she washed my feet with her tears*
> *And dried them with her hair…*

Mark and Matthew speak of an unnamed woman who anoints
Jesus with either nard or ointment. Luke tells of an unnamed
woman "who was a sinner" who bathed Jesus' feet with her tears,
anointed them with ointment, and dried them with her hair. Then,
to make things more confusing, John describes Mary of Bethany,
aka Martha's sister, anointing His feet with nard and wiping them
with her hair.

At its heart, Toronto has its homeless, its own
*misérables*, stepped over, walked around,
or worse, unseen…
I would be with them.

And so, today, I am God's Son—
My feet are tired! They feel broken.
Today, Madeleine extended
An unexpected hand—

The Foot Care Clinic coordinator, Gloria Wiebe,
from my neighbourhood parish, St. James Cathedral,
washed my feet,
cut my nails,
anointed my toes with Myrrh,
and once I was Clean,
I went into the Cathedral to pray,
to witness in my way,
by listening to Bach's *Matthäus Passion BWV 244*…

# THE SOLDIER WHO KILLED ANTON VON WEBERN

*Last question to you…*
—U.S. Army Cook, Private First Class

Raymond Norwood Bell, take care, hear me out:
Why did you shoot him?
This great composer? Innocent of all crimes?
Because he didn't come to a halt at your command?
Did you tell him—Stop! Did you shout—Stop!
He did not stop? You shot him.
Maybe he was deaf? Maybe that's what you now think?
Beethoven wrote with deaf ears.
Would you have shot him?

> —I'm telling you again. Over
> and over and over. I shouted at him!
> He wouldn't stop. He's supposed to stop.
> That's the rule. Orders are orders.
> I lost my voice crying: STOP!
> I am just a soldier, a disciplined American private!
> Doing my stint! What? Sorry.

> —Private first-class Bell! Did he walk away?

> —Sir, I told you all this already …

> —Private first-class Bell!

—Okay, okay—it was the CURFEW HOUR! He was moving, not stopping, walking down the sidewalk to his door. Then back:

       so many times! Back and forth. Back and forth...
       I cried—Stop!... And I shot!

       —Private first-class Bell! Do you realize what you've done?

       —Some officer let me listen to his music...
       Here in prison...
       That I hardly knew how to deal with.
       Different sounds.
       Hurt my ears. I'm so sorry,
       for the loss... But, from school
       I know the word "cacophony." I'm not stupid.
       I've got no experience. Limited, let's say.
       Not with that stuff.
       Cacophony. Okay.
       So, I don't deny it. I shot him.
       Sorry. I am not an experienced guy.
       I've been nowhere but here in the army.
       They don't ask me to listen to music—to cacophony—
       To be a good soldier. I'm a good soldier.
       So, during the War, I was doing my job...
       Nothing more...
       Nothing less. In the middle, I shot him.

—US Army Cook Pfc. R. Norwood Bell! Why was he shot?
You obviously don't know what happened, what we lost …
But hear my final
words to you very carefully.
This is what your victim told you about YOU:
"Indeed, man only exists insofar as he expresses himself."
You expressed yourself, sir.
You expressed yourself.

If you say so.


P.S. Soldier Bell who shot Anton von Webern was left so distraught by doing what he did in accordance with military rules of conduct that back home he hit the bottle and within ten years he died of cirrhosis of the liver…

## TSARSKOE SELO

A young poet published her first poems in the short-lived
journal *Sirius,* edited by the young Acmeist, Nikolai Gumilev.

Anna Akhmatova—a severely gorgeous,
freshly-baked poet—
content with her new book, is
strolling down the tree-shaded alleys of
Tsarskoe Selo!

Selo! Park in The Tsarist Village!
Akhmatova met Nicolas the Second
some days, weeks, or months earlier, before
her book of Acmeist poetry!

They'd met by chance?
Or maybe they'd made contact through a friend
who'd admired her book?
Or maybe to introduce her to the young Nikolai—
her future husband—leader of the Acmeists…
Maybe twice more…
At Tsarskoe Selo—where the
Tsar's family resided, in Alexander Palace, where
Anna's father's family had settled, too, because he was an
influential engineer, building a new railway from
St. Petersburg out into the wide wide world.

On a stroll and in her hand, the latest issue of *Sirius.*
She sings from her book.
Strolling among the lindens of St. Petersburg…
Is it true that the Tsar helped her?
Who knows? She's there alone in the alleys of
Tsarskoe Selo!
Strolling, singing her new poems,
paying no attention to children playing—so many
many children playing,
governed by their nannies under the lindens…

And the Tsar did not pay attention to the
pretty woman who is Akhmatova.
So many pretty girls in the park, under the lindens.
Accompanying him—his young sisters:
the Grand Duchesses Tatiana,
and the tiny Grand Duchess, Olga, who
carries a little boy, her youngest brother, who
said to Tatiana:

       "Stop. Don't touch him,
       Alexei is already worn out,
after only an hour's walk—A doctor said,
take him home… The young Grand Duchess Olga
brought him—her little brother—
almost weightless,
running all the way home.

She knows time flies—two months to Christmas—
in her girlish world—brightly coloured cards.
She paints every day. She goes to her room,
to her beloved oak easel…
Her drawing teacher—Mr. Zhukovcky—comes always at 6 pm.

I saw many of Olga's canvases in the Moscow Tretiakovka.
How could I know that by coming to Canada—to live in Toronto,
I'd be here with her—Duchess Olga—her final home—
this outstanding watercolour artist—
Olga Romanov-Kulikovski—only a few city blocks away
from where I now live, in Toronto, on the local
Avenue of the Tsars, King Street East.

## NO NAME

I've no name: two days
old—a poet birthing

an entrance
at Leningrad's
Basilievsky-Ostrovsky
Maternity Home.

For the first time,
eyes open. Into the
glare…

… a white-robed devil
wearing a cross of red,
grabs my legs (also crossed),
and beats me
on my tiny bum.

I cry—nobody cares.

Still I'm free—my brain's
neurons move lightly,
my face, dark red, turns pale pink,
meditating on genetic memories.
A grimace, a peaceful smile,
that absence of angst we babies possess,
that adults know nothing about—

symbiotic thinking
despite howling,
snuffling,
so sensual,

eyes closed or open,
it does not matter—
I am in full flight through the heavens—
I am in the reel of looping film
that I am watching
(who is the author of this scenario—me,
emerging as if I were brave,
head first into the open, vulnerable?)

back before this moment, when I was
a couple of molecules gathered into a cluster,
circling around in a waltzing sort of dance
in their time absent of time.
Hilarious! Without a present, I had a past
that was already my future! Who'd have
thought it was possible, let alone probable?

So laugh along
genetic memory! You are the last page
of my memoirs—as I ask ironically,
Well, what's to become of me?
In the next film sequence?

Will I be a fish! Blunt-nosed with a tail instead of leg?

Why am I a fish?

No! Better to be a wolf or a tiger!
Hugely absurd! Let's be serious.

An electric fish, a sun fish, a rock bass,
a scavenging catfish, a pike... a pike for our times
(what a murderous row of teeth in the snout !).
Maybe the creator gave me a stupid
beginning because my molecules
came from our damp and dank old Leningrad—
out of upheavals of ice water, the birth canals of the Neva—
connected to Baltic Sea storms—
caviar cast up on the cruel island called Vasilievsky.

The devil in white reappears
wearing the sign of the cross and
in a couple of minutes her awful rubber hands
try to stuff my baby mouth with something

like my thumb
like the little finger of a big fist!

Innocent mouth!
My God! What is it? How did I come to deserve
such a mortifying induction
into everyday life? I'm outraged!
Stop this mockery! Maybe
I'm a holy baby! A future Christ!

Or Pushkin! Or Galileo! I spit
over and over. I keep spitting,
my newborn lungs
bawling out loud enough to upend God,
my sonic scream! But then, soft

and softly in my genetic memory gently moving
fingers of an angel a saint—my brain
focusing on working my mouth—
no reels of the cinematic avant-garde
under my eyelids—

I am not a fish! I am at mama's milk, a mammal—
suckling, insatiably suckling on my suspect future…
maybe I'm Mickey Rooney, maybe Albert Einstein,
Popov the Clown, a mime, yes Marcel Marceau…
I'll become a mime of my own self… yes.

## QUEEN

*Kisses can kiss us*
                        —GERTRUDE STEIN

1

I stand on tiptoe
in the still hour of  dawn
watching the sun lap up
dew on the grass
as summer meadows
fill with stolid
black and white cows feeding.

2

By crepuscular
light
the Queen slits her eyes
and parts her lips, lethargic
amidst the magic of
smoke rings
from hand-rolled cigars
disappearing into
a looking glass
that's been poisoned by her kiss.

## BACH'S BIRTHDAY

Airborne music… a burly
animal in a beastly dance,
stiletto, staccato, on his toes all morning,
pirouetting like a studio dancer
caught in the mirror that stands
between dancers, one
imitating the other,
left right right left, rhyming, pausing,
a shared shortness of breath.

Be honest—they're hands, or,
the open palms of the same person—
a performer's hands,
the pianist—doubtless
they're flying hands
(why in such a desperate hurry?
was it Collette who said it is like
listening to the hallucinations
of a sewing machine?)
acrobatically in orbit
20, 30, 40 fingers (it seems) a deranged ordering
into a chromatic
crescendo, a quotation of
belated yet premeditated variations—
definite endings that are
always enigmatic in their resolution. ( )

Johann Sebastian Bach opens his eyes...
he is tired, he's not young,
a quarter note of sweat rolls down his nose,
unbuttoning his lace collar
he takes off his powdered wig.

"What?"

"Today's Your Birthday!"
Anna Magdalena his wife sings delightfully
off-key to the
father of her nine infants—and
hands him a crystal glass of
Liebfrauenmilch...

"Happy... Happy..."

## SOMEONE

Someone leans against my window
admiring the green Russian birch
below in my downtown parkette.

*aie...* someone
slow walks through my room
attentive, resting his hand
on my furniture,
yes, someone
is in my cubbyhole kitchen
close by the cheerful
espresso machine
as it gives up its last
orgasmic breath...

and so
again this someone
dawdles in my room,
standing with a cup in hand,
sipping—
studious before someone's portrait
hanging...

—IT IS ME—

I am so glad to seem to be seen
hanging on my own white wall

welcoming a somebody
from somewhere

for at least a couple
more days…

# GLOVES

*And then I see: my left glove*
*On my right hand…*
—ANNA AKHMATOVA

I lost my gloves, my frozen right hand
needs to shake a hand and as soon as
I come into the
room Claire smiles: "Oh I've got lots, Vladimir,
only I've only got left over left-hand gloves…"

I'd come by subway,
turned my head, thinking,
something
wrong, something lost?

"Vladimir, I'll give you
two left-hand gloves,
that'll work and
keep you warm,"
wonderfully absurd
for an absurd moment.

Someone says, so sonorous:
"Never let your right hand
know what your left hand
is doing…"

Our visit done. I decline
Claire's several left hands.
But soon, once more,
my hands are cold as I
hurry down Dale Avenue
to Castle Frank station.

I'm on a hurtling train,
wearing no gloves at all
on my cold, cold hands.
One hand beginning
to despise the other's
frailty, the other being
naturally lazy, a shirker.

Anyway, they were
only $50 for the pair,
stupid gloves,
boring brown gloves.
Why my anxiety?
It's too cold for
an anxiety yawn.

Ah-h-h! the memory,
memories. Incessant
memories: always—
of Anna Karenina after

the Prince got cold feet
and forgot his gloves
as he hurried off
to meet his fiancée—

That was the last straw: Anna
understood without being told:
those gloves left behind
stuck in her craw.
She ordered her carriage
to take her to the train,
to the train tracks…

But this is all too much!
too much for me over too little…
The key in the keyhole
*click*… and there they are,
my gloves are on my chair.
Of course they are.
Low comedy as
I wear my lost gloves around
the house so I won't lose them,
comforted, amused
by my forgetfulness
though Anna is still
lying cold in her cold grave.

## ANNA'S DREAM

Scream! A scream! Who is screaming?
An ugly old man, gnarled, grubby hands.
Surrendering? No, he is
trying to hold up the sky as
the train jolts to a stop:
a whoosh of steam, release
of the soul of a woman,
who is crawling down the wallpaper of
my bedroom, weeping…

Please, please wipe her face!
Cold, wet with red blood!
Wipe her face!

In the old train station, the ugly old man
with broken knuckles smiles,
wearing the Prince's gloves…

Anna, terrified, hadn't
heard the train
but I can hear it, I can hear as
she opens her eyes and sees
an on-coming black hole
disguised as a light.

## THE WAY TO CUT MY HAIR

Sweet scent of cheap eau de Cologne: lilac?
Those barber shops live in me.
A sickening sweetness in my childhood
that I loved.
It's how I still
get my hair cut.

I'm a school boy walking by
huge humps and mounds of Kazakh slag and coal:
we were the Soviet source
after the devastations of WWII,
KA-RA-GAN-DA.

It has the sound of a bell, of incantation—a fakir
making magic with a snake:
my mother rides by that snake to fetch the
necklace she forgot in Leningrad,
having left it on the commode
as she was hurrying off into our exile.

I go to get my long hair cut.
a teenaged Kazakh would-be hippie…

Sparkling black anthracite, a soup bowl of
smog between the slag hills…
Summer grit on the wind, swirling
down the crooked industrial road.

A pale sun pasted over Kazakhstan,
scent of the barber's lilac oils…
a sweetness so thick that
it clung to me all day,
and into the night, too,
a sweetness amidst all that slag
that still smells as if oil
had been smeared on my upper lip.

# RAIN, RAIN

Rain rain rain rain,
days and nights in supposedly sunny Moscow
—the early '60s, sharing
an umbrella with my girl.
Honking, clattering mufflers
of soot-coated cars,
the exhaust of ten-wheelers
as we walk through Gorky Street
(now Tverskaya),
my slim young wife—
elegant—her self-styled
tailored clothes—
she'll soon become a Muscovite...

She' been bred in the town where I'd been sent
to work after graduation:
in Ukraine where the climate
is much warmer than Moscow,
but all summer long, rain rain rain rain—

My old girl friend is wearing a warm wool jacket
so chic—now, she is the beautiful wife
of my friend, Juri, also an architect,
who died last year,

the confusions of time on a broken wing—

as we go down the most fashionable street past
tall store windows—streams of rain down the glass,
but there's nothing behind the glass—
the empty stores of the '70s... our hollowness
on display...

A café with hot coffee, optimistic,
we are filled with intimations of hope:
my soon-to-be wife, will come to me in Moscow;
we already have a son
and we are happy and... and suddenly—
we meet friends—
a cheerful couple coming toward us—
we're working on our dissertations at the same time—
her Asian face—bright, blonde!

Yes—We are laughing!
ABBA is the fashion—
happiness, friends!
They married... they had a son, Timur... then?
They both died... in 2014... Timur
phoned me—rain rain rain rain...
It pours. Day and night.

## WHEN WAS THIS?

*To Vasilievsky Island I am coming to die…*
—JOSEPH BRODSKY

When was this? Yesterday? Years ago?
January…
We are back by bus from the cemetery
where it was snowing incessantly.
So cold. Wind-driven snow on my father's dead face.
Blinded by sorrow I cannot see his cheeks.
Black soil and flowers fall down,
paper flowers, too,
bright, crude, artificial…
What's next?
The ritual meal? No church prayers.
Christ's resurrection forgotten.
This table is for bottles not for bread.
Then, we're home. Alone with ourselves.
Mother's on the sofa. Not weeping.
Not a tear. Talking slowly.
"I am younger than your father.
I've got five years left.
Listen my son:
I going to dye my hair.
I going to slim down.
Exercise, diet. We'll go for walks.
Along the Nevsky, take a leisurely stroll.
I will show you my Venetian cradle of the north.

Seven Line was our street. On Vasilievsky.
A third floor that had no elevator.
Still the same I'm sure…

Our light knock.
Respectful. Not threatening.
And—the current tenants ask,
"Who are you?"
She says: "I am coming to Vasilievsky Island to die…
Forgive me. Here, here
where you are, I was so alive."

## THE GOOD DOG, STRAY

Good dog, Stray, found himself a Master.
I adopted the poor creature. and
WHY NOT? Every dog down every alley
is created by God.
Not young, not a thoroughbred.
Far from it. Stray was through
and through a mongrel. A blunt snout.

Submissive temperament. Maybe some small
strain of nobility in his bones because he was
a quick learner, or maybe just street smart: easy to get
to go pee outside; actually has patrician manners,
never barks or bares his teeth at guests.
Once fed, he has a delightful
smile, especially while watching tv News.

He lifts his paw to an Honourable
friend of mine, a Master Academic
who tells him:

    —I want to change your name,
    my lovable and loving
Stray. Something more in tune with who you are:
      LET ME CALL YOU—PUSHKIN!


    —Why Pushkin?
This stray right off the angular,
narrow, and cross-hatched

streets of staid Toronto,
tar and cobble stone and cement
of a colonial military mind, streets called
Wellington, John, Richmond, Peter,
Adelaide, Dundas, King, York,
Queen (and when stymied, Avenue Road!).
But I am no longer
an architect casting a critical eye on such
matters. I am a hapless poet! Writing
in an adopted language
about an adopted dog.
And so now he is Pushkin,
my beloved, Chief Sniffer
of Curbs and Laneways:

—Arf! Woof! Arf! and Arf!
—Words! Wurds! Words! and Wurds!
My dog barks as the caravan passes on…
        Pushkin
Bring me my slippers.
It's cold, no time for going barefoot—
I'm a writer, yes, but I am not
Tolstoy who through his feet felt the Earth breathing.
I'm only a little crazy, and though
I live in a two-room
highrise apartment on King Street,
I'm going outside now to mow the weeds

despite the deep snows…with my dog Pushkin
floundering through the pure whiteness behind me
dreaming of the white sandy beaches
he has never seen back in Sochi.

## MONSIEUR PROUST

On the western side of the Right Bank,
Paris is mostly a leafy neighbourhood graced by
shimmers of gold, lovely on an autumn morning.

In search of fractured time,
brooding on life's mutations… the construction of the
Eiffel Tower, the first Métro line… spoonful's of sugar…
a love, a crush, a snub from long ago…

Divine pastries baked by his grandmother.
A child's agonies of the tongue: vanilla sugar cream melted butter…
What more? What more?
Ginger cinnamon coconut? Powdered icing? Almond?
Lost time lost taste lost childhood lost health lost love…
always the pangs of loss…

This morning he has only his cold cold body that cannot
be warmed by his fur coat: his sluggish blood circulates like anise
accompanied by an enigmatic smile and the pungent aroma of coffee.
Among his haunts, the restaurant Larue,
Café Weber, Maxim's
at 3 rue Royale… under the awnings
on this autumn morning of

cold sunbeams at play on faces in the crowd.
Pastries! Broken pastries. Broken hearts. Close to the
Lycée Cardorcet where Stéphan Mallarmé
taught English and Bizet's son, Jacques, was a classmate.
And a boyhood place by the puppet theatre

where his grandmother—who baked the
unforgettable pastries she called
MADELEINES
suffered a stroke...
listening to Bach's *Goldberg Variations* that are
played during his funeral
Mass held in Saint-Pierre de Chaillot
Chapel on Avenue Marceau...
Variations on knowing that memory
is a pastry anticipated.

## CHIROPRACTOR PAUL

I came by to visit Paul my chiropractor.
Every week at the same hour.
As usual, a five-minute wait.
Among the usual people sitting, one, two
in wheelchairs, an aging women glued to a 40" TV.
And… another patient enters, sniffing the air
of St. Michael's hospital.
An old man. Long grey matted hair. Tattered
T-shirt. Frayed shorts. An injured leg.
Wearing flip-flops and
holding a Tim Horton's Styrofoam cup,
asking for a second filler-up.
This is not Horton's. He
goes to the Spring Water cooler.
Sitting calmly I wait for
Paul, though I am in serious pain.
The man stops, smiles, asking:
     —*Are you Russian?*
I'm not surprised. My face… the bone
structure… I nod. He sits close:
     —*Hmm… Well… Baryshnikov!*
I look at him, surprised. I stare at him.
     —*Russians are a great nation! I was so young, I saw
him right here. Toronto! When? Can't recall… Fa-a-ar away…
Lo-o-ong ago… After I also tried to dance…*
     —Did you dream you were a dancer?

44

*—My dear Russian! I drank, starting in high school!*
*My name's Michael too, like him, this genius "Misha."*

—You can try dancing now, there's free classes.

*—I'm busy. My business is drinking!*
*All around me, fantastic dreams! Real fairy tales!*
*Misha visited me, sometimes… I am old. Fifty-two…*

—My son is fifty-five!"

*—Adopted by you? Sons can be a problem.*
*I was a problem for my father. But then I once thought*
*I'd like to have a son, too, a real Misha, too…*

—Michael is my real son. I stud…"

*—You're Russian. Yes you are. Don't deny it.*
*Misha s*
A door opens:

—"Vladimi-i-ir!"

—Paul. Paul. Over here. Yes, it's me, I'm in pain.

# I TURNED

I turn over on my right side, dreaming
the War—the Second… Why? Why not?
The racket of distant cannonading.
Our room on the third floor, the wood beams shaking,
wood planking buckling.  Eruptions.
Grit clouds. Dust bombs. Splinters, shards.

Aunt Manya—my father's oldest
sister, who survived the Siege—leans against the
machine gun she's set up in the open window.

Normally, she doesn't laugh. She's laughing.
And then my other Aunt—on the maternal side—Tanya,
my mother's sister, who recently died, she enters my
dream room on tiptoes carrying a bag bulging with grenades.
She is worn out. Veins popping at her temples.

How come I recognize all my dead relatives?
There's hot water running from the faucet.

I wash my hands relishing the heat, the almost burning.
I've got nothing to eat. The last piece of bread is gone.

A question: how old am I? Where am I?
Who is this silent creature huddled
in the room's corner? Me? Probably. Whose corner?

The rumpled mattress. I turn over to my left side.
My brain gets up. Goes for a short walk.
It seems to have legs. A broken foot. A hobble.
Was it a dream? Is it still a dream. I start
a morning poem… This morning?

Then I push the alarm button on the clock: 4:34.
I need more sleep, more details for the poem. Someone
Enters my dark room. I remember, yes, my dentist…
an appointment at 11 am. With a  man my age from the War.
He has a big boot. Black. Always polished.
The drill in his hand is an old
Mauser C96. He is stalking me in my room.
I will ask my aunties to look after him.
If she still has her machine gun.

## DOUBLE-GLAZED WINDOW

Why do you do it? You asked me in the past. I smiled
      I didn't know why. Just clapping, and clapping.
Applauding for something or for someone, not for myself,
someone else.
      Without bravado, just applauding something naïve,
strange, unknown rivers in flood.
      Then later, a suffering so bitter I asked the truth to come
out to clap along with me: to play at Clap! Clap! No answer.
My years crawling in the dark forest, a swan smirking
spitefully between the bullrushes at all my nightmares
through all my days.  Go away I cry but hear that all of us
are in captivity! Sleep! Sleep!
      Ask permission to get up.
                  Minus 10 today
I know from the tv News. Nevertheless,  I am enjoying
playing  with sunbeams on this side of the window pane.
My coffee cup is already empty. Drunk. I've drunk the dregs.
The soft-bottomed chair invites. Me. My keyboard waits.
      Transforms into a piano. Alas, I am not
            Svyatoslav Richter.
      Nor am I the butterfly man, Nabokov.
          However, I clap. Every morning.
Clap Clap! Yes. Applause for Vladimir—for the bright,
bitterly cold sun, for the bite of the frost, here,
      on this side of my hermetic double-glazed window!

## SEAGULL VARIATION

It was a seagull's cry
A long chain of chirling broken notes..

An echo hangs from the ceiling.
A door opens on the chill morning.

Gould pauses and goes into the backyard.
White dew, filagreed frost. His bare soles.

The seagull has killed his music.
Flapping wings in his face.

Sill absorbed, lost in The Variations.
The rank smell of dead fish on the air. He likes it...

His sorrow, The Variation's broken by vacancies.
Between notes. A pink sun smears the skyline.
He parts his lips, a pale smile, also vacant,
profound sadness.

A morning meal of shadows.
A seagull cries, a female in want...

## MY MUSE, MAYBE

Why you are stealing away
behind antique columns,
pretending to be a very plain old lady?

Because you are still as shifty
and self-serving and arrogant as ever.
Repeating useless past thoughts.

Suggesting I consider Callistratos:
what do I know about
Spartan drinking songs?

Sculpted out of Pentelic stone
straight from the Attic mountain.
Quit this charade. Confess: who are you?

Loosen your veils, sit down, have a coffee.

## A VOICE AT THE MOMA

A voice at the MOMA: "Hey!
Why not come and
see my portrait? And all the other paintings by my pal
Picasso! Hey!"

I take two steps back to look into eyes
I already know, her portrait
and a couple more canvases by Picasso, and
so here I am.

Why is she now looking away as she stands
in the doorway? She called me?
I didn't call her.
I can't get Gertrude's attention,
coming up close, smiling, trying to ingratiate myself,
a little quiet laughter—and Nothing!

A tough character,
that's for sure!
I call, rudely:

"Hey you! Word boogie
poet and acute critic!
Is it true? Did you collaborate with the Nazis?"

I am a little scared waiting for her answer.
Silence, there's always the complicity of silence.
But maybe silence can be absence? Illusion? Delusion?
Mere old age? Turning to go—I hear her voice—
clear, loud, to the point:

"YOU ARE AN IDIOT?"

## MY LUCKY LIFE

My lucky life! I say to you, to myself!
Today I met Ms. Alice Toklas here on Toronto's
very own Church Street... So unexpected!
Why's she here? I'm shy, I'm such
a modest guy. My God! I took hold of myself,
got hold of myself,
and asked bravely of the respectable lady
standing before me:
     "How are you?"
She—with her elegant aquiline nose,
big eyes squinting, adjusting
her hat's wide brim, a brim of many flowers
and birds settled and also in free fall—replied:
     "I am well."
     "You look great, Madame Toklas!" I cry,
star-struck. She says:
     "I know: I've just got a new designer—
Oleg Cassini."

*(an epigraph here, in the poem's middle—any objection?)*

*"Mr. President, I could make you as important in fashion as Jackie"*
                Oleg Cassini. *My Own Fashion*
     "Oleg?" I asked.
     "Oh yes, Oleg. Jackie Kennedy's favourite
before her untimely death from breast cancer."
     "A great loss! Oh, Madame Toklas!

I have a wonderful relic! This orange plastic
tray—with Cassini's signature on it, and also his
smart little memoir about his friendship with the President's family.
You could serve up your cookbook on this tray at tea time.
With a long-stemmed rose for each of us."

I almost weep but she doesn't hear me, busy smiling and nodding
and tipping her hat, tilting her brim full of birds
and flowers at the many passers-by who want
to talk to her here on our very own Church Street…
not far from the row of pawnshops on the east side.

# NOSTALGIA OF A DIFFERENT KIND

*—WHAT's the best food Vladimir?*
*—A millet porridge with skim milk with Bessel Margarine, 2% fat.*

I remember decades and decades ago
in a Moscow Hospital I needed to get rid of
a kidney stone, a third surgery, a third stone.

CUT IT OUT!

Renal calculus—two cm—
Navel to spine!
Stayed put in the Hospital for a month
of tedious medical investigations.
In my ward there were a couple of corpses-in-waiting.
An entourage of the middle-aged, corpulent
children circling around the beds.

Cost to me nothing. Post-Soviet Health care. Plus,
I kept getting my salary, 100%.
So that was my vacation: beached.
Slightly shabby rooms, smelling
of urine and chloroform, and shaving cologne.
A regular 9 am breakfast served from the
hallway: a plate of thin millet kasha
topped by a tiny slab of butter wrapped in gold
lamé tin foil
—instant coffee slightly sour.

One morning, a newcomer at
our table—a man from the
UK with international stones in his kidney.
He tried talking to us in half-assed Russian.
Probably tried to go into Prussia before
coming here on business. We tried to understand him:

*—I know—this porridge is made from millet—*
*A grain fed to birds.*
*I remember my mother, feeding millet to*
*my little brother's doves*
*when we lived in Nassau on the road to Suffolk.*

Nassau, Suffolk…
I was in Moscow. Now I am in Toronto,
proud to know those two words in English: —
Nassau, a street in my Kensington market district
where I shop for fresh fish, where
I buy aromatic coffee. As for Suffolk? That's the
UK city out of which Benjamin Britten,
with his friend Pears, came to Moscow
by car in 1960 to present the score of his
War Requiem to Shostakovich. But,
here in Toronto, on Suffolk Street,
I am sitting at a Timothy Café.
No requiems, no Symphony No. 9

by D.S. about war, its devastations.
My friend Ewan Whyte, eating his
muffin (bran? blueberry?), asks me:

—*What's your favourite food Vladimir?*
—*Millet porridge with skim milk, with a wedge of Bessel Margarine 2% fat.*

In this life I shall suffer a new kidney stone.
And another. And another.
Because life is good if there is enough porridge.

## REMNANTS

Remnants of my father…What I did not know
while we were in exile in Kazakhstan.
Both my parents deported to work
that cold stormy land.
The Stalinist call! Work! Work sets you free!

The remnants are mysterious, tempting.
Three things— So soft and so
beautiful, a leather pilot's hat.
My father's? That made sense but
I didn't know for sure. It was not
the custom in my family to ask questions.
The usual answers were— Son, my son,
it was so long ago. So long. So long now.

Still, I wear it—his magic hat.
My father the flyer, grounded in the gulag.
Too big for me.
And a briefcase is the second remnant.
A bloodless brown colour,
a word on the metal
lock—strange—"Keller"—
Also on the hat's clasp—"Keller"—
(Who or what was Keller?)

A square case, flat, thin, as flat
as the empty years—
but what had he done
before all that?
Begore the crushing hours
of hard labour and boredom?
A real pilot's glasses.
I admired myself in the mirror:
an alien from Pluto
who turned out to be born
much later as Spiderman
in Kazakhstan. By the way,
where are they now? Those glasses?
Disappeared. Like everything
else from long ago. Disappeared.
(dreaded word).

My father's "Fotocor" USSR camera—
Flashing magnesium!
I used it to photograph the girl
who came to help my mother;
she'd lost her parents through exile,
but she'd found me, instead, the boy
who snatched her image out
of the air, adjusting her pose,

tilting her head, easing her right hand open,
trying to catch the light on
her small breasts, her high cheek bones,
making her mine as best I could,
which she knew and resented.

# CARROT PURÉE

It is very dark after dusk. The window
in my boyhood bedroom
is intrigued by the intricacies of frost
as art on its glass. I am
intrigued also, as I sit
drawing with my coloured
pencils while preparing a short
commentary on three of Pushkin's
poems for tomorrow's class. But—oh—
my mother is not here. She should
be here. She must have finished
her work at the office hours ago.
Hours ago. Where is she?

> *Frost and Sun! A marvellous day!*
> *But you're still sleeping, my lazy beauty…*

I repeat these words many times. These plain words.

I've done already all my household chores.
The cast-iron stove is lit and burning.
I can see fire through the air holes,
So I play cheerfully; not a thought
about our hard exiled life.
Read again my lesson and wait for mother.

"Vladimir!"
She enters on a cloud of frozen air.
Looks triumphant.
Oh my God! She has a huge canvas bag!
So heavy!
"Hello, my dear. Don't worry!
I had to help one of our friends."

"What is this?"
"Carrots! Frozen. A bit of food for us."
"Carrots? Oh, mama. That's our only food?"

"Hey boy! CARROT PURÉE! Delicious, so healthy!"
"Okay, okay…"

Despite my doubtful mind—

   *The frost and Sun! A marvelous day!*

The sliced and chopped orange chunks
are whirling in the aluminum pan,
bubbling, dancing, softening, wanting to be
eaten by this hungry schoolboy and his
mother, who's so tired after her long work shift.

   *Frost and Sun! A marvelous day!*
   *But you're still sleeping, my lazy beauty…*

"Vladimir! What did you say? LAZY? No my dear!
Pushkin loved women of very noble ambitions…
Some of them translated his beloved Byron.
Because he had a problem with English.
His women were not lazy.
They were educated ladies preparing for the Sorbonne
or Cambridge, they were like our Leningrad in spirit…
Or they became intimate friends or maybe the
wives of the Decembrists…"

"Who were these Decembrists, mama?"

"You'll learn about history in next year's class…"

Our food was ready, steaming on the plate…

"Mama… this is delicious?"
"Yes, my dear. It has a French name, *purée*…"
"Mama! Last month you brought us frozen potatoes:
*kartofel'noye pyure*… I love our language:

mashed potatoes…

*Frost and Sun! A marvelous day!*

*morkov'noye pyure.*"

## DON'T STARE AT ME

Don't stare at me, don't scare yourself,
don't think of how it will be when you reach my age.
I'm ninety-five and still alive.
I've closed my eyes, I don't want to know how
guests react to the sight of me. I just say thanks
to those who come out of the blue and visit me,
and I know—nothing's changed: green trees,
pellucid air, more pollution and the same politicians,
while the same winds are blowing through Van Gogh's mills,
though I will say this about the future: I hope Fukushima
is not the fashion—also Oppenheimer
of the atomic bomb, and Sakharov, cousin to
the H-bomb, and second cousin to the international
teams behind our whirling cosmic satellites…

Oh! Let Glory be! Let us consort out of compassion
for each other on fields of grass where soldiers
may be marching in lock-step (after all, that is
what soldiers are trained to do, row upon row)
but now, now they are singing poignant love songs to
a beardless Christ who is shaking the hand of Mohamed…

## CLOUDS

Heavy clouds tumble through a low
hanging light pregnant and waiting
to break water and to have their bellies
torn open to provide evidence of
God's Holy Grace through new crops
that will become vintage as we haul breath
into our lungs yearning for the faith that
will keep us trying to earn our wings…

## A SEPARATE WORLD

LENINGRAD, our Venice of the north:
At eye-level I see
a Confectionary Store, a tall and wide
glass window and behind the glass,
so many bright wrappers and jackets
on my beloved candies with funny
animals and beasts in full colour,
sculpted chocolate figures, and eggs,
here in the Leningrad I left when I was three
years old holding mama's hand, very much
a Leningrad woman in her tailored striped jacket,
her beret at a tilt on her brunette hair—
trying to pick up our pace but I have come
to a slow halt because I cannot tear my eyes
away from the divine apparition of chocolates,
caramels, cookies, chocolate cherries, more more more…
    —Mama! please, buy me this candy!
this and this and this! Or just this! This caramel. What,
no chocolate? Harmful. You mustn't say that,
you mustn't, you'll break my child's heart.
        —you have something like this at home, my son.
        —no, no mama! I want them now.
        —I told you, you've got the same at home.
        —no-o! NO! (I cry!) Ah-a! There's no
        marshmallow at home!

—Buy it mama! I want the pastila-a-a!
—calm down, please!
—ah-h! ah-h!
Mama touches my elbow…
—control yourself!


Oh my God! My sister. I see my sister, her weepy
eyes, we're sitting beside each other inside a bus,
empty except in the middle, where there's a
coffin, my mother, her beret askew…

## SCYTHING AS WE GO

*If I spit, they will take my spit and frame it as great art.*
—PABLO PICASSO

A barefoot bearded peasant
holds a scythe in his hands.
… a wandering tramp:
With his eyes closed he says he can see,
eyes open he says he is blind; also,
sensitive to high winds he forecasts constant rain…
hears a train whistle: says the train is
connected to the morgue. Not by him. No, he says he
is just a tramp along for the ride. In this life.
Certainly, he is no Count, no thinker nor activist,
no music lover. Does he know Goldenweiser?
Of course not. Why should he?
The young Landowska, or Bach?
Maybe. Who knows what he knows, what he has
picked up along the way.?
Scything is what he sometimes works at.
Yes, he is a someone from nowhere
with a scythe… a man unto
himself… wetting his thumb,
running it along the blade… yes, yes…
so that the cut will be clean.

A thin book falls to
the hardwood floor—
Chekhov's short stories…

On a summer evening
in a Moscow suburb where
today my sister lives… she sees
that a tramp is on her street,
shouldering a scythe,
and as such in the city,
he appears ridiculous,
but my sister breaks into tears
and can't stop weeping and,
inexplicably, she can't stop
laughing through
her weeping till she falls
asleep, dead tired.

Clean air near the Istra, far
from a local smelting plant,
close by Christ's Monastery
of the New Jerusalem,
a gentle wind lifts Chekhov's spirits
as he sits on the porch of his Yalta house,

the Crimean sun bright but somehow
pale, even pallid… as he watches a tramp
lay down his scythe to sit in the shade
of the garden cypress. The tramp calls out
and asks Chekhov for a drink of water.
Chekhov gets up to get the water,
filled with trepidation, foreboding,
though the tramp has given
him a sign, a smiling thumbs up.

# VLADIMIR AZAROV
## WITH
## EXILE EDITIONS

In *On "The Death of Ivan Ilyich,"* Azarov imagines himself exchanging personalities with Tolstoy's great character, Ivan Ilyich, who – as the story progresses – becomes more and more introspective and emotional while he ponders the reason for his own agonizing illness and death. In doing so, Azarov enlarges his personal experience by giving the most simple and most ordinary and therefore most terrible death of a close friend a mythic dimension... Azarov's fear of death leaves him and, as Tolstoy suggested, the terror attached to death itself disappears.

This is a bilingual book, with an English version, and Russian text on the flip side following a cover in Russian.

Few moments, certainly few speeches, in the 20th century so radically altered the flow of international events and specifically the direction of Russian history as Nikita Khrushchev's 1956 attack on the cult of Joseph Stalin. Overnight, a society under the lock and key of ideology and the eye of a secret police was sprung loose, entering into a period that has since come to be known as "The Thaw." Suddenly, citizens like the young Moscow architect, Vladimir Azarov, were free to read banned Russian writers like Solzhenitsyn, to attend concerts by stars like Marlene Dietrich, and free to go not only to Berlin but on to Paris. Azarov has written 26 monologues, each devoted to recollecting sunburst moments of freedom, moments of awareness when millions of people were suddenly coming in from the great cold of Stalin's years of terror.

A wonderful look at Soviet-era life as witnessed from the edge of the empire, this book is comprised of letters, poems, and prose pieces that together create a narrative. Through an entirely original form, Vladimir Azarov, who trained to be an architect in Moscow during Stalin's Iron Curtain years, begins with a simple exploratory exchange of letters between him and a faceless bureaucrat during his days overseeing the design and construction of the Soviet Embassy in the isolated republic of Mongolia. What follows is an unfolding sequence that finds Azarov meeting a remarkable Mongolian woman and later discovering the memoirs of one of Russia's greatest poets, Anna Akhmatova, and eventually revealing an unlikely love story between the Mongolian woman and Akhmatova's son. This enthralling account serves as both a cultural study and an exploration of the human condition.

Providing a rare and creative sense of authority's various faces, this collection of poems travels from intellectual and artistic power to philosophical, military, and imperial power; and, above all, personal influence. The verse introduces the persuasiveness, complexities, and intrigues of "table talk" – a European tradition of informed and enlightened conversation that has virtually disappeared from the experience of North American culture. Commanding and informed in their own sense of purpose, these pieces evince a gentle curiosity for greatness, creating an engaging portrait of simple humanity, powerful minds, and memorable ideas.

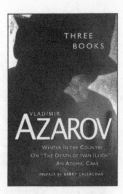

In the first of three books, *Winter in the Country*, Azarov imagines the enormous presence of the great poet, Pushkin, and his influence on the development of the modern Russian psyche. In *On "The Death of Ivan Ilyich"* he imagines himself exchanging personalities with Tolstoy's great character, Ivan Ilyich, who suffered and died from a terminal illness. In doing so, he enlarges his own personal experience by giving the death of a close friend a mythic dimension. In the third book, *An Atomic Cake*, he explores a Moscow world of wild contradictions, surreal social hysteria, and periods of massive malaise, all occurring under the cloud of atomic bomb testing. This is when he met a passionate computer specialist whose father had witnessed the American atomic testing at Bikini Atoll. Together, trying to make sense of such a world, they talked, imagining into existence the spirit of Rita Hayworth as she rode on the side of the bomb in her negligée.

Vladimir Azarov was a child of the Soviet Kazakhstan steppe. When his mother discovered that he had a slight curvature of the spine, with her own loving humour she nicknamed him Richie, after Richard III, the 14th century English king, himself crooked, made famous as a monster by Shakespeare. At the same time Azarov suffered a vision-altering wound to his eye that transformed the way he perceived the world, both real and imagined. The wound eventually healed and, as he grew up feeling a wry kinship to the king, his bent eye became that of a visionary, of an artist who was a convention-breaking architect, and finally as a poet, not writing in Russian, but in the King's English. When, not long ago, the actual bones of Richard III were found under a parking lot in Leicester town, Azarov – now in his 80s living in Toronto, and remembering his kinship by name – envisioned the archeological dig and re-interment of the bones, and he became one in his mind with the reputation-renovated and redeemed king. He became, at last, Richie-Richard III, being sung to on a rainy day, over a new grave, by medieval knights.

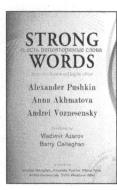

Celebrating three Russian literary greats – Alexander Pushkin, Anna Akhmatova, and Andrei Voznesenski – this collection of their writing presents new translations of a combined 34 poems and includes both Russian and English text. A handful of masterful illustrations are also included, opening an artistic dialogue with the poems and the reader. Similar to many other writers and artists throughout history, Akhmatova was influenced and inspired by Pushkin, and her canon of work has also endured and been acclaimed for its artistic integrity. Voznesenski was a poet and writer who had been referred to by Robert Lowell as "one of the greatest living poets in any language." These three master poets are brought together with translations that engage their many complexities. Six poems are presented from Pushkin, 22 from Akhmatova, and six from Voznesenski.

An unyielding fever of 103, the Sochi Olympics, and a state of inspirational semi-delirium came together as Vladimir Azarov sat in front of his television, and images swirled in his mind like a waltzing kaleidoscope. Memories from decades past were triggered as the Pussy Riot girls were being whipped by Cossacks. Marilyn Monroe of *Some Like It Hot* became his muse while he composed recollections: his first trip to Sochi in 1962; sitting with Henry Moore at his home in Much Haddam; discussing verisimilitudes with Pasolini, art with Frank O'Hara, film and acting with Leni Riefenstahl; shock at terrorists killing Israelis in Munich. As the 2014 Games ended, his fever abated. This remarkable book of poems arose from those two weeks.

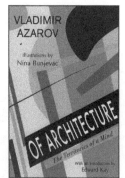

A lively collection populated by historical icons, each poem a story about the potency of imagination, territories, border-crossings of the mind – among them: the madness of a king who wants to be a swan; Michelangelo chiselling a heart that beats into his David; Tsar Peter with his three pet dwarfs acting as generals in the army; Vera Zasulich who became the world's first woman terrorist; Robinson Crusoe hunting for the footprints of Friday; Michael Jackson pretending he is Marcel Marceau as he woos Marlene Dietrich in Paris…

Illustrations by Nina Bunjevac. Introduction by Edward Kay.

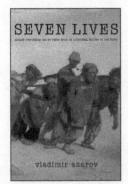

Vladimir Azarov grew up and came to maturity during a time in the Soviet Union when penal camps and the secret police were ubiquitous. But the one great truth that he and the world learned from all the great Russian writers, and that he learned in his own life in political exile, is that almost everything can be taken from an individual but his or her story, his or her undying and unyielding sense of self. No matter what, the self perseveres, even in the most perverse and punishing circumstances. Azarov, in his own plainspoken voice, has composed seven stories about seven lives that are marvellously moving in their seeming simplicity, their actual depth. *Seven Lives* is Vladimir Azarov's childhood experiences of Soviet life transformed into a poetic witnessing.

*Night Out* celebrates that which holds the world together. From Van Gogh and Gauguin's tempestuous relationship in Arles to the dichotomies of modern-day Tokyo where the bustle of a giant metropolis is set against the Zen calm of monks and cathedral builders, the worlds of architecture and poetry are united in this collection.

  *Night Out* is a tribute to the architects and visionaries who have had a hand in shaping Vladimir Azarov's inner landscape.

Publisher's note: In 2017, I met with the then-Director of the Ontario Arts Council, to discuss why Exile Editions' funding was, unexpectedly, being cut. One of three picayune points was "Why are you publishing Vladimir Azarov? This is now six books – which, to us means that 'You are not giving space to other poets.'"

  Perplexed, I explained that a core goal for Exile was not only to establish an author (we've brought out over 200 books by first-time published and emerginging writers in our 50 years) but, so very important to a writer's career, we have been committed to building bodies of work, and whenever possible to creating for each writer a presence within the Canadian literary milieu. And that is what we did with, and for, Vladimir Azarov. *The Long Ago Poems,* his 12th book with Exile (and following four collections with Book*Hug) will be his final – failing health ended a wonderful, insightful, and what should be to all writers, an inspiring career.

As for the Ontario Arts Council, 10 years ago their assault on established cultural practice was well underway with an emphasis on "Priority Groups." They were, and still are, engaging in social engineering: telling publishers what was acceptable, if they expected to be funded. (Which is also telling readers what they need to be reading.)

  The pursuit of excellence, as a prime consideration for its own sake, has been replaced by politics and sociology. They, like the Canada Council for the Arts, have targeted publishers like Exile, who have a long-standing history and tradition rooted in quality, *no strings attached.* Vladimir, an elderly white man, was not their priority. But he was one of ours.

At Exile, we are here, doing what we have always have done, and that is publishing writers without any consideration as to what they look like, what their background is, what their sexual or gender preference is – or for what scores Priority Groups points in cultural agency check boxes. And not surprisingly, our publishing activities are no longer supported by the Ontario Arts Council.